hands on display

Rhona Whiteford and Jim Fitzsimmons

Line drawings by Martin Wansborough

Acknowledgements

The authors and publishers would like to thank the Headteacher, Mrs. J. Charnley, and also Mrs. C. Prescott and the rest of the staff and children of St. David's C.of E. Primary School, Haigh, near Wigan, Lancashire, for their hard work and co-operation.

They would also like to thank Revd. R. Crankshaw, and the P.C.C. of St. Anne's Church, Beech Hill, Wigan, for their kind co-operation and help.

Special thanks are given to Laura Whiteford and Charlie Whiteford for contributions to artwork.

Skeletons and moving figures (see page 7)

First published in 1996 by BELAIR PUBLICATIONS LIMITED
Albert House, Apex Business Centre, Boscombe Road, Dunstable, LU5 4RL, United Kingdom.

© 1996 Rhona Whiteford and Jim Fitzsimmons
Reprinted 1998

Series editor: Robyn Gordon   Design: Lynn Hooker
Photography: Kelvin Freeman and Sam Hill   Illustrations: Martin Wansborough

Printed in Singapore by Craft Print

ISBN: 0 94788 239-1

Contents

INTRODUCTION

Hands on Display has been compiled with a view not only to presenting ways of displaying children's work in an aesthetic way, but to giving ideas for many of the other visual and three-dimensional aspects of teaching which stimulate children's curiosity, reinforce what they are learning, and encourage them to take an active part in the learning process. The ideas are intended to encourage children's natural curiosity as they are invited to peer into displays, lift flaps or open boxes, or to try experiments and test equipment.

A good display will be referred to constantly. It will stimulate further ideas, and may well lead to other areas of investigation. An interesting display table will be well used, and the children should be encouraged to take a pride in the displays, and help to keep things tidy whenever necessary for others to enjoy and use.

If you involve the children as much as possible at the planning stage, and in decisions such as location, choice of backing papers and the arrangement of the displays, you can instill a sense of ownership, and encourage a feeling of responsibility and care.

The displays can be adapted and simplified to suit particular needs as necessary and, with just a little alteration, many of the basic ideas can be used to provide support for many different areas of the curriculum other than the ones illustrated.

We have included ways of organising information within the classroom, ideas for displaying collections, for making efficient and attractive workstations, for creating role play areas, and ways of making simple theatres. There are also inspirations for making areas within the school for visitors - where they will feel welcome and comfortable.

We hope that by using these ideas your displays will become an integral part of the busy and stimulating working environment of your classroom, enriching the children's experience and encouraging an imaginative and enthusiastic approach to learning.

Rhona Whiteford and Jim Fitzsimmons

MOVING PARTS

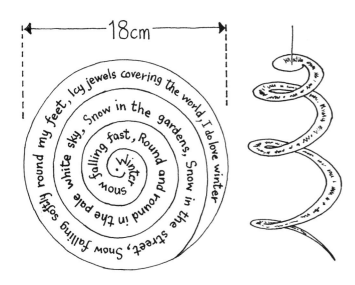

SPIRAL POEM

Starting at the edge, draw a spiral on a circle of white card (approx. 18cm in diameter). A simple spiral with only a few circles is best, to enable easy reading of the poem.

After composing their poem on a separate sheet (to allow for drafting and revising), the children can copy the finished poem on to the spiral, starting at the centre and working towards the outer edge.

After the spiral is cut, the edges can be decorated with sequins and glitter, and then the poems hung on a branch, supported in a bucket of sand.

Display in a corner of the classroom where the children can read the poems as the spirals twist and turn.

WORD WHEEL

Cut out a circle, 12cm in diameter, and mark eight equal sections. In each section, write a verb which will end in a chosen way, for example, with 'ed' or 'ing'. Make sure the words do not need double letters in the middle when they change.

Cut a strip of card, 12cm x 4cm, and place behind the card circle so that the end of the strip covers the centre point. Now push the paper fastener through the centre of the card circle, making sure that the end of the card strip is also pierced at the same time. (The other end of the card strip will now extend beyond the edge of the circle.) Lay the word wheel flat on the table and, using a felt-tip pen, write the chosen ending on the card, as shown.

Now as the wheel is turned, new words can be made by adding the chosen ending, for example, kiss - kissing.

Clowns are...
funny
hilarious
sad
tall
short
plump
bouncing
acrobats
tumblers
leaping
great
marvellous

Wells for clean water
Books for schools.
Medicines for the people.
Baby food.
Homes to live in
Seeds and rainy seasons
Tools to work with
HAPPINESS

My Christmas list
A sit down
Well behaved children
A robot that irons
World peace
More trees growing
by Mis Whiteford

BOUNCY BODY WORD LIST

Cut out templates as shown. Children can add details and features such as eyes, skin colour and hair. After making an initial draft on paper, the children can then take a piece of art paper and fold it like a concertina. The folds can be used to write words for a word list, or for poems and stories.

Assemble the body by gluing the head and arms to the top of the concertina-ed sheet, folded and held in place with a paper clip or plastic clothes peg, so that the children have to remove the clip or peg to reveal what is written inside.

15cm

← 30cm →

fold →

Ben

Sue

STORY WINDOWS

Cut out a square of card, 15cm x 15cm. In the middle of this, cut out two rectangles 9cm x 3cm as shown. Decorate the large square to look like a viewfinder or a television set.

Next, take a strip of card and thread through the card square as shown. Mark the strip into sections the same width as the window on the card frame. Remove the paper strip.

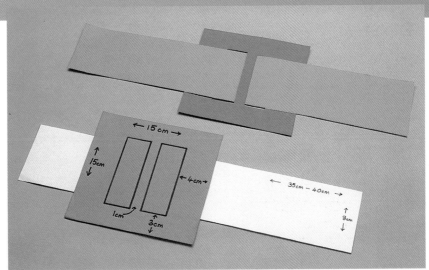

The children can now draw pictures in each section to tell their story, and then slide the strip along through the card frame and tell the story as each picture appears.

SKELETONS AND MOVING FIGURES

Children can be given a photocopy of a skeleton or human figure to colour and cut out. Use the paper fasteners to join the parts of the skeleton/figure together at those places where there are joints. The number of joints to be identified can be limited for younger children, or increased for older ones.

Groups of these figures can be used as part of a class display to show a variety of different joints or parts of the body, or they can be used during a class discussion to enable individual children to locate and name the various parts. When using as part of a display, simply attach the figures (using adhesive putty) at the centre of the reverse of the body so that the children can move the arms and legs as they wish.

A large figure or skeleton could also be mounted on a board together with a set of labels as part of a classroom display so that the children can try to identify and label different body parts.
(SEE PHOTOGRAPH ON PAGE 2)

MOVING TEDDY BEAR

Cut out head, body shape, two arms and two legs from card. Paint, colour or collage the various parts, and then punch two sets of holes in the body and at the top of each arm and leg. One set of holes in each arm and leg is for the paper fasteners and the other for string.

Fix the arms and legs in position with the paper fasteners, making sure they are not too tight and that they all swing freely. With the arms and legs in a 'relaxed' position, fasten a length of string or thread horizontally between the second set of holes in the arms, and do the same between the two holes in the legs, as shown.

Next, join these two horizontal threads with a vertical thread fastened to the middle of each, and make sure that this extends below the body of the bear as shown. Pulling this vertical thread will make the bear's arms and legs move.

The same technique can be used for a variety of different characters or animals.

SUBTRACTION CARDS

Take two rectangles of white card (each 15cm x 10cm) and cut one in half as shown. Decide on the equation you want to show, for example, *6-3=3*.

Take the complete card and draw a set with three members on it. Keep the three members over to the left hand side of the set, as shown. Now take one half of the other card and place it over the right hand side of the first card and fasten in place with a paper fastener. Complete the set by extending the ring on to this top card. Draw in the extra members of the set in this other half to show a set of six (see diagram).

Write the sum *6-3* on the left side of the bottom card and on the top card write in the 'equals' sign and an empty answer box. Swing the top card up to reveal the right of the bottom card and complete the equation to read *6-3=3*.

The children can practise number bonds and subtraction using these cards with an instant check on their answers.

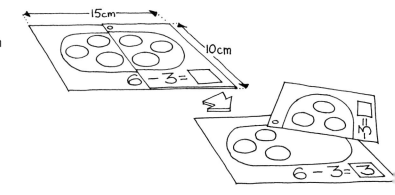

GROWING PICTURES

Take a strip of card or cartridge paper (approx. 40cm x 10cm) and fold as shown. Lay the folded strip on a flat surface and draw a picture of a creature such as a snake, crocodile or caterpillar. The creature will appear quite short and fat.

Now open up the folded sheet to reveal a gap in the body of the creature. Join the two halves by extending the lines. The picture can be coloured and decorated.

Fold the picture as before. Now the children can write on the left hand side, for example, *'A very...'*, and on the right hand side *'...slithery snake'*. Open up the card and in the middle space they can add, for example, *'...very long slippery...'*, so that the picture changes from *'A very slithery snake'* - to *'A very very long slippery slithery snake'*, each time the card is opened.

These cards are useful for helping children to understand opposites, and the use of language in mathematics such as *long/short, high/low, tall/short*.

The cards can also be used vertically, and the children can draw buildings, people, plants and trees.

HUMPTY DUMPTY

Cut out an oval shape and a rectangle shape from stiff white card. Decorate the oval by drawing in features with paints or felt-tip pens, and use scraps of material and wool to make it look like Humpty Dumpty.

Paint the rectangle to look like a wall, using small rectangular pieces of sponge to print brick patterns. When this is dry, join Humpty Dumpty to the wall with a paper fastener.

The children will enjoy reciting the nursery rhyme and watching Humpty fall off at the end.

STORY WHEELS

RAPUNZEL

Cut out two circles of card, one white, 17cm in diameter, and one coloured, 15cm in diameter. Cut a window in the circle of coloured card, as shown.

Next, take the white card circle and divide into segments (four for younger children, or up to eight - as shown - for older ones). Place the coloured card in the centre of the white card and fasten together with a brass paper fastener.

The children will need to think about how they will divide their story between the sections and, once they have done this, they can either write or draw through the window on to the white card beneath. As each segment is filled, they move to the next one to continue. When all the sections are complete, the story is read by turning the white card to reveal each section through the window.

Top card, Base card

15 cm diameter

centre marked

6cm
1½cm 4cm

cut out

17cm diameter

centre marked

Divide base into ¼, ½, or ⅛ s

Fit two cards together with paper clip

Rapunzel
A fairy tale
Read it here
Once a wicked witch stole a lovely baby girl and locked her in a tower
by Laura

I'm coming

Turn the wheels

CITRUS FRUIT

An adaptation of the above idea can be used for a Harvest Festival display. The children write poems on to photocopied sheets showing a cross-section of an orange, each line of the poem to be written in the segments. Make a circular folder from yellow card and mount the poem inside this, using a brass fastener to act as a pivot, so that the poem can be turned as it is read.

Colour the outside of the folders to look like oranges, and hang them from a branch of a tree fastened to the wall, or supported in a container. The children lift the fruit-shaped cover to reveal the cross-section of fruit and the poem inside.

HINGED SNAKE

Copy the shape as shown for each of the body parts on to stiff card or cartridge paper. The snake can be as long or short as required by varying the number of parts.

It can be as large or small as required by varying the size of each part, so that this can be either an individual or class project.

Each part of the snake is decorated using paints, crayons or felt-tip pens. Cut out a head as shown and decorate this also.

Finally, all the pieces are fastened together with paper fasteners to create the snake with a body that can be positioned in many different ways. Phrases which describe the snake, or its actions, can be written on the body sections, with one phrase per section.

SPLIT BOOKS

You will need: A5 size sheets of white paper and an A5 rectangle of card

Decide how many pages you want in your book, then cut the A5 sheets of paper into three equal parts as shown. Staple these to the rectangle of card. Draw different characters on each of the pages. Because the pages are split into three parts, the head will be on the top part, the body on the middle, and the legs on the bottom part. The children can then colour and decorate each page.

The books can be used for descriptive writing, where the child chooses three different parts to create a new character.

For older children, you can provide a variety of different beginnings, middles and endings of stories on the three sections. The children would then write a story with the three elements contained in it.

A GROWING BEANSTALK

Take a rectangle of card 30cm x 20cm. Let the children decorate this as shown, and cut a slit 8cm wide near the bottom of the card in the middle, as shown.

Next, on a strip of card 7cm x 30cm the children draw their beanstalk. Using adhesive tape, attach another thin strip of card on the reverse close to the slit to hold the beanstalk card in place. Then thread the beanstalk card through the slit at the back, so that the picture of the beanstalk appears to grow out of the ground at the front. (See reverse view in the photograph.)

SOUNDS WINDMILL

Make or buy several large windmills.

Glue a card circle to the centre of each windmill showing a consonant blend or vowel digraph. Fix labels to the sails showing words which contain these blends.

Display in a decorated tin or plastic seaside bucket weighted with sand.

ORGANISING INFORMATION

ROTAS
DRINK MONITORS

Cut a piece of blue card to the required size, and decorate as shown with cut-out shapes or felt-tip pens.

To make the crate, cut a rectangle of black or dark blue card long enough to fit across the bottom of the first card, and fold in two lengthways. Cut out a row of rectangles along the folded side, then open out and glue or staple this to the bottom of the first card as shown, to create a pocket.

Cut out bottle shapes from white card, making sure they are large enough to be seen above the level of the crate, and adding details such as labels and bottle tops. The names of the children who are the drink monitors are written on the labels and the bottles are slotted into the crate to show who is in charge for that day.

Make a storage crate for other class names from a painted shoebox with strips of card as divisions.

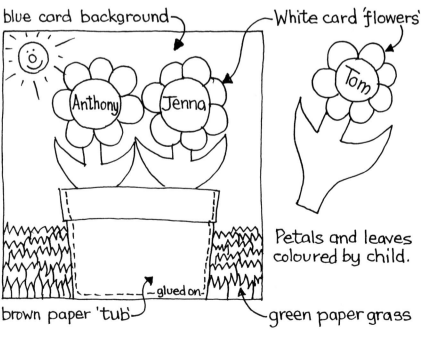

blue card background

White card 'flowers'

Petals and leaves coloured by child.

brown paper 'tub'

green paper grass

GARDEN MONITORS

Garden monitors can be shown in the same way but with a variation of design. Choose suitable colours of card and paper, and this time cut out a large plant pot as shown, and also flower shapes. Children can colour and decorate their own flower, and write their name in the centre.
Staple or glue the plant pot on to the backing sheet to make a pocket, as for the crate above. The children's flowers are placed in the pot to show who is responsible for the school or class garden.

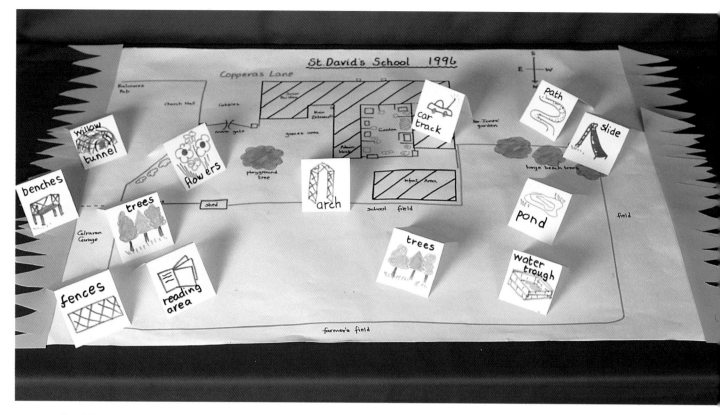

CLOSE-UP ON PLANNING

You will need a map of the area to be planned. This can be a printed map, or one drawn by the children. It can be either an imaginary situation, or part of a project, for example, to improve school grounds.

Now have a brainstorming session with the children to gather ideas as to the sort of features they want to see introduced. These ideas are then drawn on to folded pieces of card as shown.

Each group can have the opportunity of siting their chosen features on the map in the places they want them, and discuss the advantages and disadvantages. The cards allow features to be moved easily until a final plan, agreed by all, is achieved.

CAR RACE

Cut a strip of coloured card 18cm x 106cm. Divide this lengthwise into three tracks with a felt-tip pen.

Decorate a 3cm strip at the start as shown and then mark off twenty spaces 5cm long with a 'Finish' strip at the other end. Mark these spaces 1-20. Three children take turns to throw the dice and move their toy cars along the track.

At the end of the race, they put their cars in order on the rostrum created from a shoe box lid with a card cut-out 'Winners' sign glued or stapled along the back edge, and ordinal numbers 1st, 2nd and 3rd along the front edges as shown. This gives practice in number sequencing and positioning.

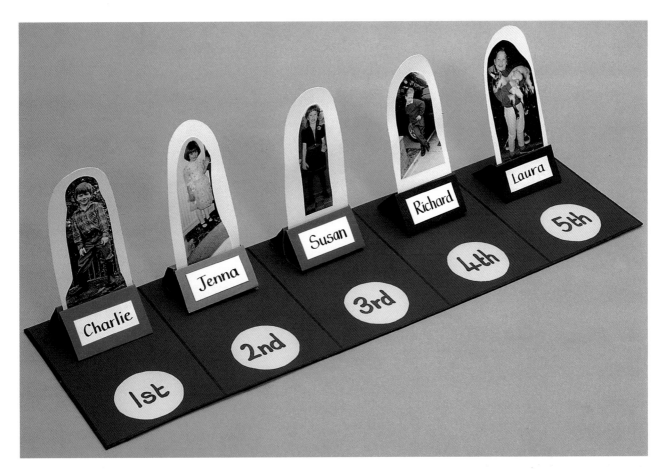

WHICH ORDER?

Cut out whole body photographs (or just head photographs) of each child, or ask them to draw themselves, and mount the pictures on white card.

Cut a strip of card 6cm x 20cm and mark off as shown below. Fold along the lines to make a stand for each picture - which is then slotted in the top.

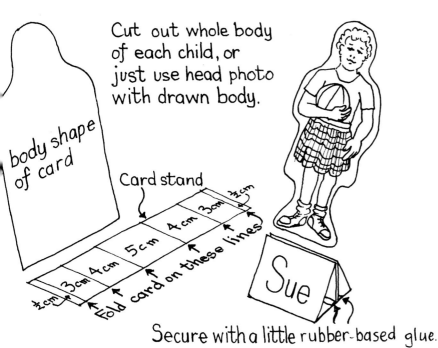

Cut out whole body of each child, or just use head photo with drawn body.

body shape of card

Card stand

½cm 3cm 4cm 5cm 4cm 3cm ½cm

Fold card on these lines

Sue

Secure with a little rubber-based glue.

Cut strips of paper, and with felt-tip pens mark out number lines and ordinal number placings. The children can then put the figures on to the line and record the positions they put them in.

For older children you could make a list of placings, and the children could put the pictures in the correct positions on the line. Remember to include reverse number lines as well.

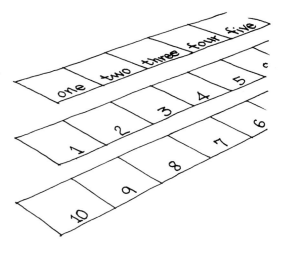

one two three four five

1 2 3 4 5 6

7 8

9

10

MATCHING ORDER

Cut strips of coloured card and mark out the number lines as shown. Write the numbers on plastic or polystyrene beakers with felt-tip pen, or glue on numbers cut out from card. The children then have to match the cups to the same number on the number line.

Alternatively, glue a set of numbered cups on to a number line as shown and make another set of cups to go over the top. (A small bead glued to the top of each fixed cup will stop the children pressing the matching cups right down where they may get stuck.)

As an extension, the children could be asked to match folded word cards, as well as placing the correct number of small items (such as beads, buttons or shells) next to the cups in order to help with recognition of number, word and quantity.

Match name cards too

| one | two | three | four |

FISH FOR WORDS AND SOUNDS

Cut a strip of white card 1m x 15cm. Let the children decorate both sides with underwater illustrations of plant and animal life. Then cut out some fish shapes, 10cm long, from coloured or white card. Using felt-tip pen, write words containing consonant blends or vowel digraphs, then place a paper clip on the tail of each fish as shown.

Attach lengths of string to the garden canes (which can be covered with paper, as shown) and tie a small magnet on the end of each to make the fishing rods. Join the two ends of the paper strip with paperclips to form the pond, and put the fish in, word side up. The children can then choose a letter blend or sound, and fish for the words which contain it. The first one to get all their words is the winner.

3D BOOKS

For the triangular or square shaped 'book', take a strip of paper and fold into the required number of equal sides. The children write on each separate (outward facing) page and decorate with a picture or border.

Alternatively, take the required number of separate sheets and glue them together. The children write on one side of the paper and then decorate with a picture or a border. Mount on coloured card and assemble into shape. Number the sides. Display the writing so that the children have easy access, and can pick up the 3D shapes to read them.

For the cylinder shape, take a long strip of card and form into a cylinder large enough to take the pages of writing. Alternatively, a long strip of paper can be used which has been marked off into page-sized sections, and numbered. Join as a cylinder when the writing is complete.

For the star book, mount the writing on folded rectangles of card and asssemble as a book by numbering and stapling the pages together.

Make sure the front and back covers are left blank. Open the book wide until the front cover meets the back cover. Staple or glue these two together as shown, and the book will make a star shape.

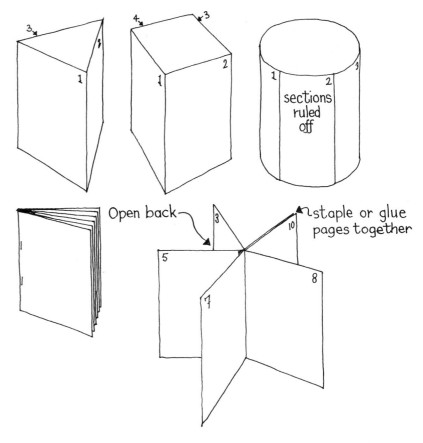

PICTORIAL STORY BOARD

Cover a board of required size with a sheet of felt. Divide it into six equal sections, as shown, using a thick felt-tip marker or coloured adhesive tape.

Cut labels to size from white card and fix to the board with Velcro. Use your own or children's drawings (or old books or magazine pictures) for illustrations of characters and places. Cover with adhesive plastic film for protection if desired.

Draw or stamp clock shapes showing different times when the story takes place.

Write simple phrases such as:

a big explosion	*a dangerous journey*	*ind treasure map*
go on treasure hunt	*visit castle*	*see strange lights*

to give ideas for the main events, and make cards with a variety of openings and endings for the bottom two sections.

If wished, cover all the cards with the protective plastic film, and on the back of each card place a strip of Velcro. Store each set of cards in boxes next to the board. The children can work in small groups, or individually, to create their stories.

Older children can use the same idea, but instead of a storyboard, keep a sheet of paper to hand with a store of pencils or felt-tip pens nearby, so that as they go about their work the children can write their ideas over a period of time. The class or group can then be brought together for a brainstorming session to sort out all the ideas and tidy up the list.

Using these ideas, a group of children can write a story and illustrate it. Make it into a book, record the story on tape, and then place it in the class library for others to read. Older children will also love to do this for the very youngest children in school.

MENU BOARD

Take a piece of board or stiff card and paint or cover it with activity paper.

Leaving a space of A4 size in the middle, create a border all around the edge of the board. Use food pictures cut from magazines, or print with cross-sections of fruit and vegetables and, when dry, cover with protective plastic film.

Each day's menu could be written by the children and attached to the middle of the board with an adhesive putty. Display in a prominent place for all to see.

This would also make an attractive menu for a school café.

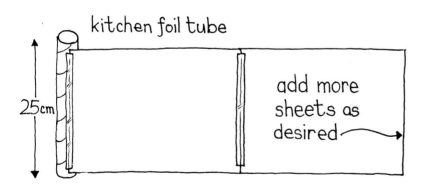

SCROLLS

Use glue or adhesive tape to join sheets of A4 paper together to make a long strip - or use a roll of art paper.

The children can decorate the paper after they have completed their writing or drawing by adding, for example, a border. For an antique effect, brush the edges of the paper with cold tea.

Using glue or adhesive tape, join the ends of the paper to cardboard tubes, which can also be decorated if desired.

MAP BOARD

Use a board made of thick card or wood, cut to required size, and paint or attach a map. If, for example, you want the map to show the countries of Europe, you will need an outline of Europe which shows the borders of each country.

Place a strip of Velcro in each country, then draw or paint the national flags with the name of the country written underneath. Mount these on card and cover with protective plastic film. Attach the hooked Velcro strip on to the back of each flag. The children then try to match the correct flag to each country on the map.

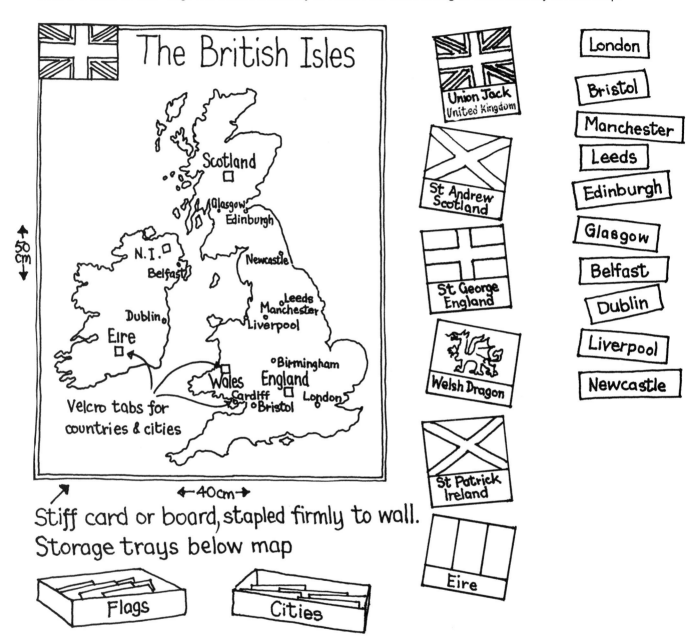

This can be made into a game if the children time each other. The one who gets most correct in the shortest time is the winner.

The board can be used for any topic requiring maps - such as food sources, holiday destinations, sites of historical events, or geographical features. The board can also be used for positions of planets in the solar system, naming parts of the body or a vehicle, or for labelling equipment used in an experiment.

DATE AND WEATHER BOARD

Take a rectangle of stiff card or board of the required size, and paint it, or cover with a brightly coloured activity paper or cloth. Decorate with cut-out shapes or potato prints. Next, cut out strips of card and write on them as shown.

TODAY IS   THE DATE IS   THE WEATHER IS

Put these in position on the board as shown, then see how much space is left. Cut the next cards to size to fit in the space. You will need cards showing:

- numbers 1-31
- 12 cards showing the months of the year
- seven cards showing the days of the week
- six weather cards with symbols as shown

Attach strips of Velcro to the weather board where the cards are to go, and attach the hooked Velcro on to the back of the cards. The children can be responsible for changing the day and date, and for recording the type of weather each day.

SOUNDS WASHING LINE

Cut out large letter shapes as shown - approx. 15cm for small letters, and 30cm for the tall letters. (The bigger they are, the better the effect will be.)

Start with the basic letter sounds for young children and build up to the consonant blends and vowel digraphs for older children. Write words containing the relevant letters, blends and digraphs on pieces of card 30cm x 15cm.

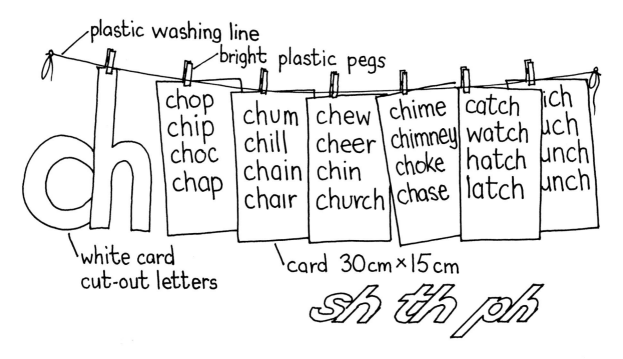

Fasten the line along a wall or across a corner (bearing in mind the need for safety), and fix the letters and cards in place, using brightly coloured pegs.

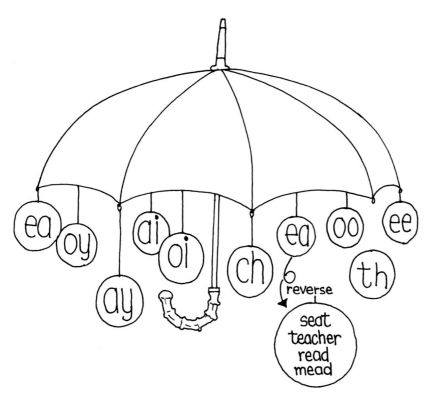

SOUNDS UMBRELLAS

Suspend a large umbrella (for example, a golfing umbrella) from the ceiling, by means of a cup hook and string or twine. Cut card shapes, as shown, to the required size.

Write a consonant blend on the front, and words containing the blend on the back. Hang these from the spokes of the umbrella as a sounds mobile.

You could use several small children's umbrellas grouped together to highlight a particular set of sounds, or alternatively use the idea to display times tables.

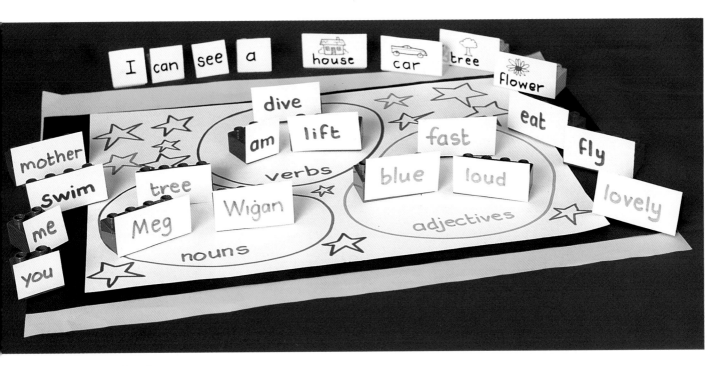

WORD BLOCKS

Obtain plastic or wooden building blocks. Cut cards to size to fit over the longest side of the blocks. Select key words for sentence construction or to help with a reading scheme. Write the chosen words with or without an illustration, as shown. The children can choose the words they want in order to make sentences for copying, or to help them with imaginative writing.

Older children can also use this idea to help them with punctuation and grammar. Make sets of words as shown and ask the children to sort all the nouns, verbs and adjectives into different sets. Use these in sentences.

FAN MAIL

Cut a rectangle of coloured paper to the desired size, and pleat this to make the fan.

A letter or poem, or writing of any kind, can be written in lines on each flat surface. Staple the bottom edge as shown and add a twist of parcel ribbon.

Decorate the edge of the fan with felt-tip pens, glitter, sequins or feathers.

WALL DICTIONARY

You will need: sheet of cloth 96cm x 84cm approx.
material of a contrasting colour
two dowel rods 86cm long
braid

Sew a 2cm hem all around the large sheet of cloth and loop the material top and bottom to take the dowel rod, using 6cm for each loop. This makes the back sheet. Excluding the loops, this should now be 80cm square.

Cut five strips 10cm x 82cm from the material of a contrasting colour and sew a 1cm hem all round. (The strips will now be 8cm x 80cm.) Attach these horizontally to the back sheet, leaving a 8cm gap between each row. To create the pockets, sew vertically from top to bottom on the back sheet to create six equal pockets per row.

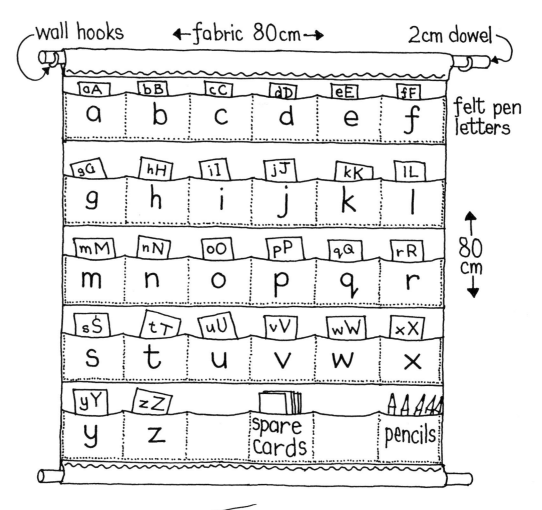

Using a marker pen, write a letter of the alphabet on the front of each pocket, then push the dowelling rods into the loops at the top and bottom of the back sheet and decorate with braid and tassels if required. Finally, fasten string to the ends of the top rod and hang on the wall. Place a strip of white card in each pocket and use the spare pockets at the bottom to store pencils and spare cards.

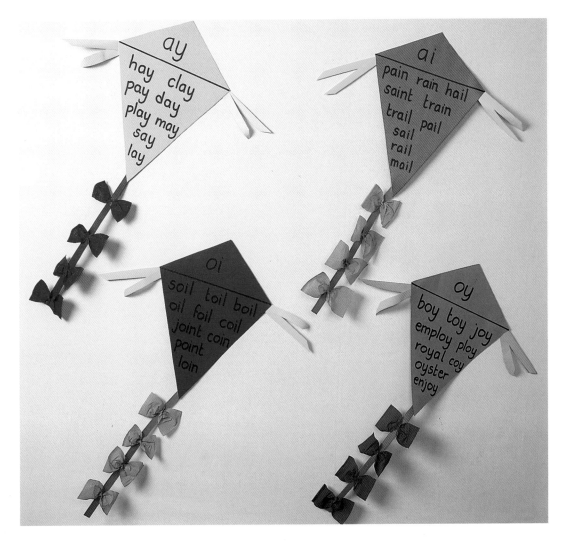

SOUNDS KITES

Cut out large kite shapes to required size from card or activity paper. (If necessary, reinforce the shapes with cross pieces and verticals using garden canes to prevent curling.)

Attach strips of card (or string) and paper bows, as shown, and choose a sound (or blend of sounds) for each kite. Write the letters of the sound at the top of the kite, and in the space below write words which contain that sound. Display these on a wall where the children can refer to them easily.

PANDORA'S BOX

Find small boxes which would be suitable for this activity - for example, boxes that hold freezer bags or cling film. Paint the boxes or cover them with bright activity paper.

Take a strip of paper 40cm long and slightly less wide than the box, and fold into 2cm pleats.

Make small word banks by using these boxes in a variety of ways, for example:
- write different kinds of words on the paper, such as verbs, nouns or adjectives
- write words or phrases suitable for a particular kind of story.

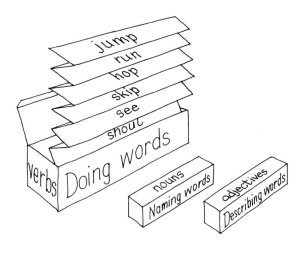

Using adhesive tape, attach the pleated list to the base inside the box and push the pleats down into the box. The lid can be held in place with a small strip of Velcro.

25

A Single Fold Niche - see text below

A FOLDING NICHE

A focal point for a display can be created using a niche. The simplest way to enclose the space is to take a sheet of corrugated cardboard, 80cm x 30cm, or any size suitable to your needs, and score and fold as shown in the diagram.

The card will stand freely when folded and the surface will hold pictures or drawings, and if you place the folded card on to a flat surface (such as a small table or cupboard top), models or pieces of equipment can be placed in front to create a small display.

A SINGLE FOLD NICHE

Just one fold in a sheet of stiff card can create an interesting corner anywhere in a room. It can be left plain or decorated with cut-out coloured paper, paint or silver foil (see photograph above).

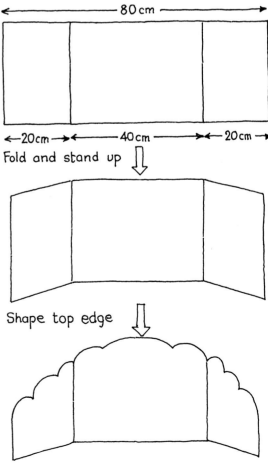

80 cm

20cm 40cm 20cm

Fold and stand up

Shape top edge

26

ZIGZAG NICHES

Join foil sheets or coloured card with adhesive tape to create a zigzag niche. Individual models can be separated easily using this method of display.

DIORAMAS

Cut a length of corrugated card and fold into three equal parts. Shape the top of each part as shown.

Curve the corrugated card as shown and staple or pin the middle point of each curved section to a back wall.

The point created at the fold of each section can be held in place with adhesive putty to create three curved compartments. This will enable the different parts of any display to be kept separate if desired.

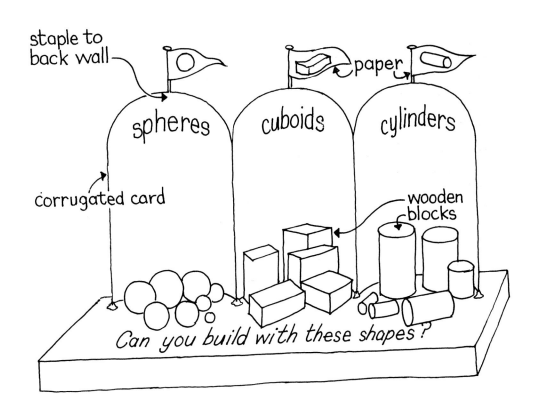

USING A PICTURE AS A BACKGROUND FOR MODELS

A large picture can decorate the sheet of corrugated card to create a suitable background for models, toys or games.

Cut and shape the corrugated card as before, and make a background picture with cut-out shapes, or children's drawings, to create a suitable backdrop. The models are then placed in front.

To prevent the backdrop from falling over or collapsing if a group of children are gathered around the display, you can fix two tall coffee tins with lids (and filled with sand) to the back of the corrugated card with glue. This will help to keep it upright and also help to keep the curve.

Using a picture as a background for models

The diorama can also be used as a backdrop to give instructions for an activity, with the necessary materials ranged in front of it - as shown below.

BOX OF DELIGHTS

Paint shoe boxes (or cover them with coloured activity paper) and position them as desired. Join the boxes together using glue or adhesive tape, and then use them to display collections of small items, as shown.

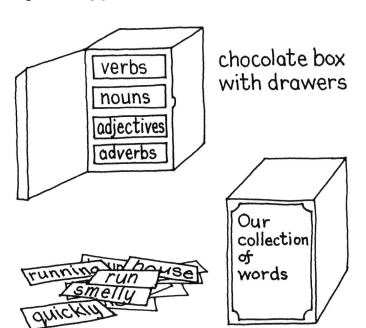

chocolate box
with drawers

verbs
nouns
adjectives
adverbs

Our
collection
of
words

running
run
house
smelly
quickly

WORD CHEST

You will need: a chocolate box with set of drawers, as shown .

Cover any brand names on the box and label as appropriate. The box can be used as a word chest - perhaps with one provided for each group or table.

Alternatively, use the box for housing mini-collections assembled during topic work.

29

SEASONS BOXES

You will need: a shoe box
blue Cellophane or pale blue tissue
Christmas and birthday cards
old calendars

Remove the lid of the shoe box and cut a viewing hole in one end as shown. Cut chosen scenes from the cards and glue at intervals down each side of the inside of the box. The cut-outs should be taller and narrower nearest the sides, with smaller features near the middle, allowing the eye to see through to the far end of the box, where you can glue a suitable picture.

Finally, cover the top of the box with blue Cellophane or tissue paper. The children can then look through the viewing hole to see inside.

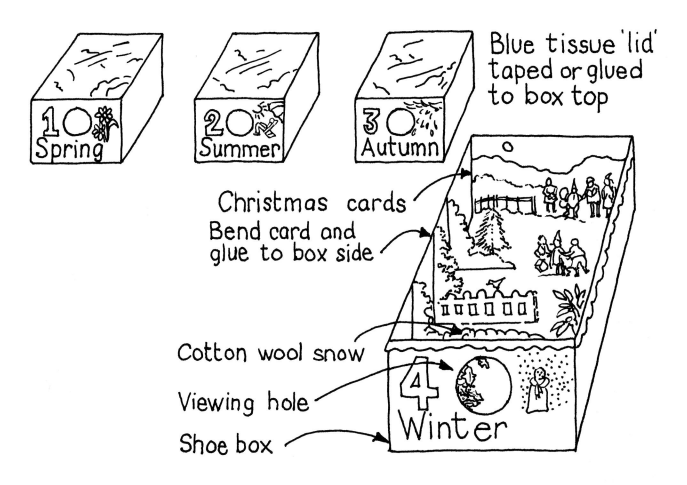

Blue tissue 'lid' taped or glued to box top

Christmas cards
Bend card and glue to box side

Cotton wool snow

Viewing hole

Shoe box

Make a box for each of the seasons, and decorate each one with large letters cut from card, spelling out the name of the seasons. Choose appropriate colours and designs on the outside to allow the children to become familiar with these visual clues, and the spelling of the words.

Numbering the boxes will also allow recognition of the sequence of the seasons during the year.

VIEWING TUBES FOR COLLECTIONS

Cover the outside of tins (either dried milk, coffee or baby milk tins) with brightly coloured activity paper, and then stack as shown. Hold together by binding with coloured adhesive tape.

This can be used to display collections of small items or used as 'sounds' tubes.

At the bottom of each tube the letters which make a particular sound are glued, and a list of words which contain that sound are kept inside for reference, and can be added to by the children as they come across them and use them.

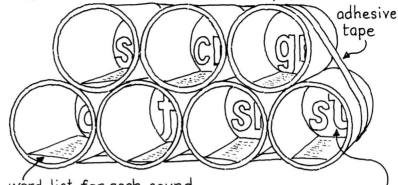

Pigeon-hole viewing tubes –
Coffee tins, covered with coloured paper.

adhesive tape

word list for each sound

cut-out paper letters glued to back of tin

ch

choc
chip
chum
chap
chill
chin

MINIATURE WORLD

Cut away the front of a shoe box as shown and paint and decorate the outside with cut-paper snowflakes for a winter scene.

Cut out pictures from old cards and calendars and glue these to the inside of the box. Place in some small bare twigs as trees (or use cut-out tree shapes) held in place with Plasticine. Use a strip of silver foil as a frozen stream, and then cover the base of the box with cotton wool piled in drifts.

Finally, put in some plastic cake decoration figures, or toy figures, to complete the scene.
The idea can be adapted to make a mini world for any season of the year, or to make a scene in support of any topic.

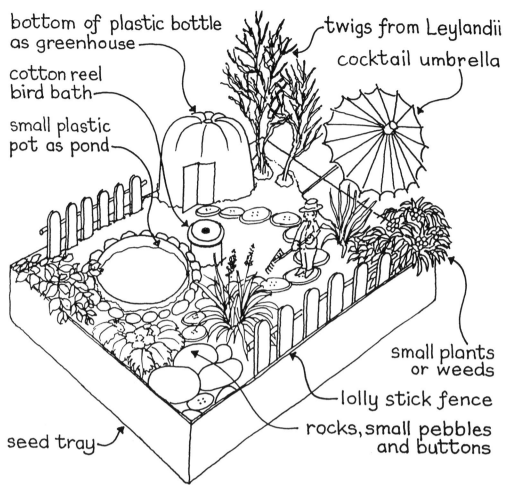

bottom of plastic bottle as greenhouse

cotton reel bird bath

small plastic pot as pond

twigs from Leylandii

cocktail umbrella

small plants or weeds

lolly stick fence

rocks, small pebbles and buttons

seed tray

MINIATURE GARDENS
You will need:

  seed tray or shallow dish
  small pebbles
  coloured stones
  small sticks (e.g. lolly sticks)
  plastic bottle
  margarine tub
  twigs, compost
  selection of small plants

Fill a small seed tray or shallow dish with compost. Give the children a sheet of paper and ask them to plan their garden.

Encourage group discussion about what features they want in it, and then ask the children to draw a plan of where they want the features to be. Next, discuss the drawn plan and talk about the way they are going to turn their ideas into reality.

Discuss the materials required to make the pond, or a fence, or how to make a green house, or what should be used for the path. When the children have assembled all the things they need for their garden, they can begin to construct it.

Put the plants in first and encourage talk about scale. If possible, include some small plastic figures or ornaments.

Trays can be decorated with patterns using acrylic paint or water paint mixed with PVA glue.

The children can plan any garden or environment in this way, and it provides lots of opportunity for problem-solving.

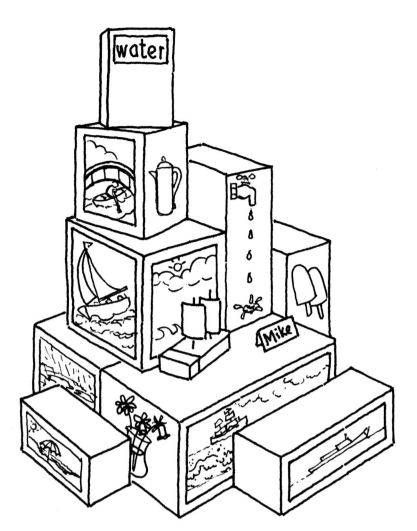

ISLAND DISPLAYS

Collect a set of boxes of various sizes, and paint or cover these with coloured activity paper. Stack them as shown in the centre of an open space.

The various sizes of boxes will allow you to create both horizontal and vertical display surfaces. These can be used to display written work, pictures or models.

By placing the boxes in an open space the children can move around them, thus increasing the amount of display space available, and allowing viewing of the display from a variety of different angles.

cardboard box with deep lid, coloured art wools in balls inside.

WOOL DISPENSER
You will need:
> tins (either baby milk or coffee tins)
>> with plastic lids
> coloured activity paper
> balls of wool

Paint or cover the tins with paper the same colour as the wool that each is to hold. Make a hole in the plastic lid, put the ball of wool inside the tin and replace the lid after you have threaded the end of the wool through the hole.

You could put the cans of wool into a decorated box with holes, as shown, and use it as a wool dispenser (the tins stop the wool becoming tangled), or simply leave the tins grouped together in a shallow tray or box lid.

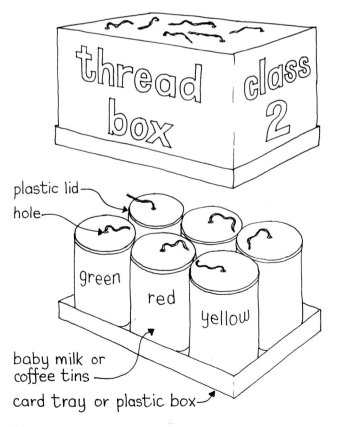

plastic lid

hole

baby milk or coffee tins

card tray or plastic box

RUSTIC SHELF

Take one or two small wooden fruit boxes obtainable from greengrocers or farm shops, and use these to create rustic shelving within a large display.

Stand the boxes on a display surface or nail them to the wall or pinboard, and use the insides and the top surfaces to create 3D displays. **(See photographs above, and also on page 69.)**

WISH WANDS

Roll up tightly an A3 sheet of activity paper, to make a wand. Cut three lengths of coloured foil 3cm x 25cm. The children write their wishes on the white side of the foil.

Next, lay the foil strips flat, one on top of the other, foil side up, and with the wishes starting from the left. Fold over the ends on the left-hand side, making sure you do not obscure any of the wishes, and tuck them, as one, into the end of the wand. Use a little glue to secure them in place.

Cut thinner strips of coloured foil and curl them. Add these to the top of the wand for decoration, as shown. (As the children wave their 'wish wands', their secret wishes are carried away on the breeze!)

FEELY BOX

Turn a large box on its side so that the flaps are positioned as shown. Glue a card strip on to one of the flaps as shown, and fix Velcro strips to this and the other flap. This will allow an object to be placed inside the box.

Now cut an arm hole in the top side of the box. Paint and decorate the box with potato prints, sponge prints, or cut-out paper shapes, as shown.

Each child can put his/her arm into the hole to try to guess what the objects are.

FEELY BAG

Take a large bag with elasticated top (or drawstring) and decorate the outside with sponge prints, for example, stars and moons. Place a shoe box inside and put a mystery object inside that.

Each child puts a hand into the bag and has to guess what the object in the shoe box is by feeling it. Make sure that the neck of the bag is kept gathered so that the children cannot peep inside.

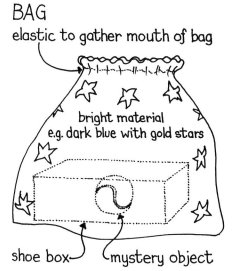

BAG
elastic to gather mouth of bag

bright material
e.g. dark blue with gold stars

shoe box — mystery object

TUBE
fabric tube with
elastic gathering

large card
cylinder

paint or decorate with foil

FEELY TUBE

For small objects you can use a cylinder shape made from card or a cardboard tube. Make sure it is large enough for a child's clenched fist to pass through easily. Paint or decorate with foil or tissue paper shapes, then fix a sleeve of material to the top of the tube with an elastic gathering at the top. Children use this in the same way as before to guess what the object inside is.

WORKSTATIONS

There are many cupboards and trolleys designed for storage within schools, and available from educational suppliers, but if these prove to be too expensive, it is possible to create your own storage space. Re-position cupboards to create a storage and display area. If possible, remove the doors from older cupboards to make objects more accessible. You can store items on the shelves of these cupboards in wire trays, redundant school trays, or even large cardboard box lids.

Each tray and each shelf should be labelled clearly with contents lists for each so that individual items can be checked and returned to the right place.

Store boxes of workcards or relevant books close by, and decorate the area with suitable pictures and posters to create a stimulating environment. Finally, encourage the children to keep everything in a neat and tidy state at all times.

LEGO CONSTRUCTION BANK
Stand corrugated card (one metre wide) around the top of a table on three sides, and secure with adhesive tape. The card can be stapled to a back wall to secure it. Attach Lego posters, project cards and labels as shown. Place the small containers on the table and put in the different Lego pieces.

Store base boards close by, and have a box of project cards for the children to work from. Encourage them to sort the Lego pieces into the correct boxes when they have finished using them.

LEGO DISPLAY
Set up the display area close by the work area. Place the completed models on the display with individual labels fixed with adhesive putty.

MUSIC CORNER - SORTING SOUNDS

Using the space above a cupboard or table (placed against a wall), cut a shaped backdrop from coloured activity paper, and label and decorate with note characters cut from black paper as shown.

Fill two coffee tins with sand, then paint or cover with paper. Place these on the table-top or cupboard in front of the backdrop.

Fix a thin plank of wood on the top of the tins with adhesive putty and display a collection of instruments on the shelf. In the space below the shelf, position four plastic containers and label as illustrated.

Ask the children to sort the instruments according to how the sound is made when they are played.

MUSICAL INSTRUMENTS

Paint or cover boxes with coloured activity paper. Place them side by side and cut a length of corrugated card, shaped as shown for the backdrop. Cut out large note shapes from black card, and letters for the labels from coloured card.

Display home-made musical instruments, and label as appropriate.

PAINTING CORNER

Fix corrugated card around three sides of a paper trolley or table to form a booth on top, and use this to display examples of painting techniques.

If desired, cover the artwork examples with protective plastic film to prevent damage and splashes.
Use a large tin or plastic jar to hold paintbrushes and spread paper over the surface of the trolley.

Plastic containers of water can be positioned near the back of the painting corner to avoid spilling. Include a paint palette or whatever art material is being used.

BOX STORAGE

If you do not have a paper trolley, you can make your own box storage using six strong cardboard boxes taped together. The wine bottle boxes found in supermarkets are ideal for this.

Fold in the opened flaps for extra strength and, using wide adhesive tape, fasten them all together. Cover the whole with a patterned plastic film.

If you wish, you could make these into work areas by placing a sheet of thick card or thin chipboard on the top. You could make several of these and set up individual painting areas around the classroom.

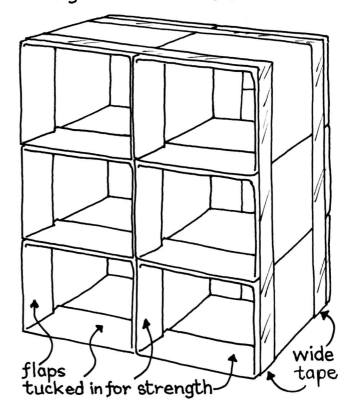

Strong cardboard wine bottle boxes

flaps tucked in for strength

wide tape

LISTENING BOOTHS

You will need: corrugated card
large boxes
wide adhesive tape

You will need a good expanse of wall and two heavy cupboards to secure the corrugated card and create the booths.

Position the two cupboards where you wish the booths to be, and start off by stapling the end of the corrugated card to the side of the first cupboard. Create the booths as shown by folding and stapling the card to the wall as you go along, then finally to the second cupboard. Use the wide adhesive tape to secure the partition walls to the floor as illustrated.

Take the large cardboard boxes and paint or cover with coloured activity paper. Put one in each booth. Decorate each booth with appropriate posters or artwork, and place a tape recorder and tapes in each for the children to listen to.

These booths can be used for listening to music or story tapes, or can be adapted to make quiet writing corners for individual children.

SOMETHING SPECIAL

TREASURE BOX

In a well-ventilated area, spray the inside of egg boxes with gold or silver spray paint and leave to dry. Paint the outside of the egg boxes with bright poster paint, and decorate with labels, paint, pictures, glitter, large sequins, etc.

To complete their treasure boxes, the children should choose six items, whatever they wish - the only stipulation being that they must be interesting, unusual or special, and that they must fit into the box.

Once they have made their choices, the children can be encouraged to take turns to say why they chose the things they did.

SOMETHING SPECIAL BOX

Take a flat shallow box (which might be a lady's dress box, or a shirt box) and paint or line the inside. When dry, decorate the outside as shown, using paints and glitter, and make a large label to read: 'Look in here to see something special'.

The box can be placed flat on a table or cupboard, or fixed to the wall. Place inside any good pieces of written work or artwork that you want to highlight for that week.

THEATRES

FOLDING THEATRE
(The advantage of this theatre is that it can be folded flat for easy storage.)

Cut the required shape from an A4 sheet of thick paper (or thin card) as shown. The children can paint the backdrop directly on to the back of the theatre, or attach different scenes as required.

The puppets are children's pictures cut from old cards, attached to long straws, and introduced from the side, as shown.

PRISM THEATRE
Take a sheet of card 50cm x 16cm and score and fold it into sections 16cm long. This will leave a 2cm strip at one end which should be scored and folded also.

Use a craft knife to cut a window in the side next to this 2cm strip, leaving a border of 4cm along the top, 1cm down each side, and 5cm along the bottom.

Draw or paint a scene on the two 'back' sections and assemble the theatre by tucking the opposite end of the card behind the 2cm flap, secured with a paperclip.

Make cut-out puppets and fix a long straw to the top or side of each one. This will enable the children to introduce the characters through the open top of the theatre or at the front of the theatre.

THEATRE BOOK

Make a book by folding and stapling several sheets of card together. Glue the back and front covers together to make a star book (see page 17). Draw the scenery on each double-page spread, and cut the edge to shape as shown.

Cut out or draw characters for the play and fix to long straws or garden canes. The children turn the pages to change the scenery and tell the story.

Younger children will enjoy using the table-top theatre, and older children can be encouraged to write the story or play, make the theatre book and perform the play for the younger ones.

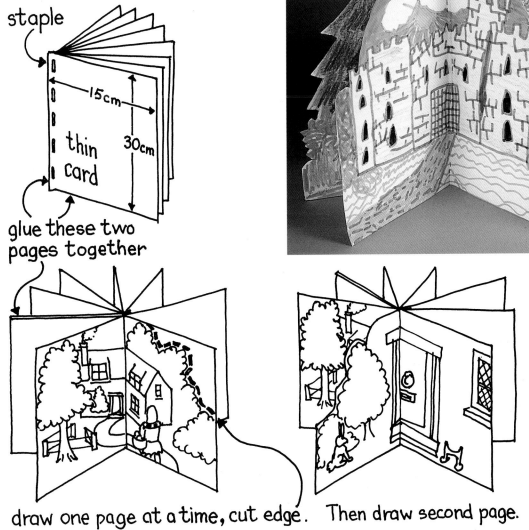

staple

15cm

30cm

thin card

glue these two pages together

draw one page at a time, cut edge. Then draw second page.

SHADOW THEATRE

You will need: strong thick cardboard l.4m x 40cm
black card
garden canes
good quality tracing paper, or thin white cloth
light source
adhesive tape

Cut a rectangle of thick cardboard 1.4m x 40cm. Measure 20cm in from each end and score and fold to make two sides. Cut out a large rectangle from the central section and cover this with the tracing paper or fine white cloth to make the screen.

Set up the shadow theatre on a table, making sure the sides are placed at a shallow angle to the screen and secured to the table with adhesive tape. The puppets are silhouette shapes of the characters attached to sticks as shown.

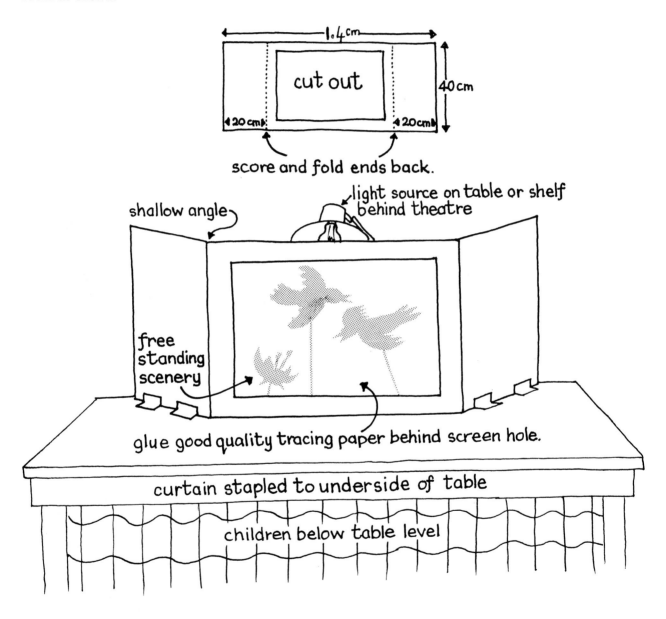

The children sit under the table hidden by curtains or a piece of draped material, and a light source is positioned on a cupboard or table behind the screen to enable shadows to be cast on it when the children hold the puppets in between. They will need to experiment to find the best way to hold the puppets, and also to find out how close they need to hold them to the screen in order to make the best shadows.

44

BOTTLE GARDEN

Take a large fish bowl or transparent plastic water bottle and put in a layer of pebbles and gravel. Cover this with a deeper layer of compost. Water the compost and leave for about an hour.

Fasten a fork and a spoon to the small canes with tight rubber bands and use these to plant the houseplants and cuttings. (You could also use an old barbecue fork, which is ideal.)

When the bottle is planted to your satisfaction, gently water again and cover the opening with cling film. This will keep the moisture in and create a 'mini climate' inside the bowl.

To add a little interest you can, if you wish, put in dinosaur figures or small decorative ornaments.

small canes

rubber bands

old kitchen utensils

old barbecue fork

assorted small houseplants /cuttings

pebbles, gravel and good compost

DIY FOR BIRDS

You will need: wooden pole   square of chipboard
wooden edging strip   nails
drawing pins   string
collection of nest-building materials   food and water

Take the square of chipboard and nail it to the wooden pole. Tack the edging strip around the board. Leave a gap in the edging strip so that uneaten food can be cleared out frequently. (A few holes drilled in the birdtable tray will allow rainwater to drain away.)

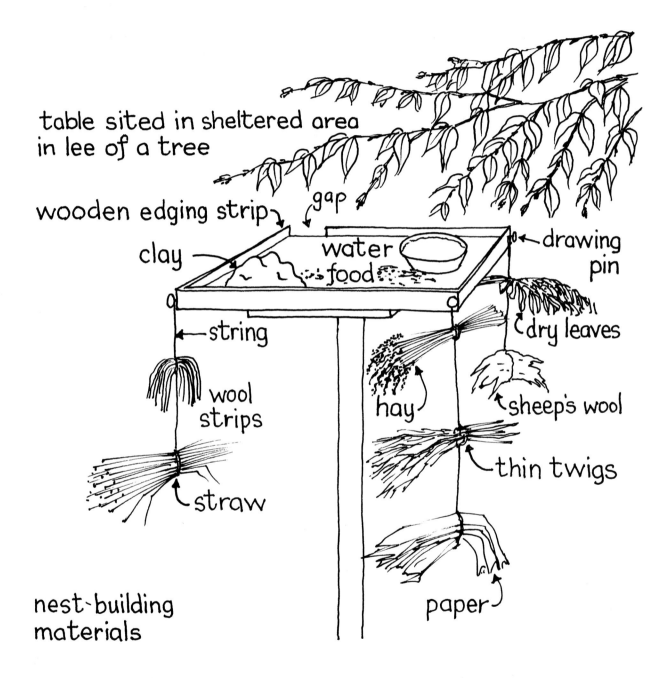

table sited in sheltered area in lee of a tree

wooden edging strip

gap

clay

water

food

drawing pin

string

wool strips

hay

dry leaves

sheep's wool

thin twigs

straw

paper

nest-building materials

Position the bird table in a sheltered spot under a tree, making sure that cats or vermin cannot reach it. Attach the nest-building materials at each corner by suspending them from strings fixed with drawing pins as shown. On top of the bird table provide food and water and some soft clay.

D.I.Y. for birds						
Bird	preferred materials for nesting					
	string	wool	straw	paper	leaves	twigs
Blackbird						
Thrush						
Starling						
Wren						

Keep a record of the birds that visit the table and note which birds use which materials in their nest-building. Make a chart like the one shown and the children can take turns to observe and record. This activity is best done during the spring term when most birds are actively engaged in nest-building.

NEST BUILDING

Fold a strip of green paper to make a concertina. Staple one end and open out into a fan shape. Fasten to a work surface. Collect a variety of common nest-building materials and place them in separate large tubs as shown. Provide a large tray or shallow box lid for the children to work on, and also try to obtain an old abandoned nest as an example for the children to copy. Display this on a plinth made from a painted or paper-covered food tin. The children are to try and build a nest using the materials provided.

Older children might like to try building with just one hand - since the birds can only use their beaks. As they do try to build a nest, encourage the children to think about how long it takes for the birds to build their homes, and encourage greater awareness and concern for the protection of birds, nests and eggs.

A BIRD CAFÉ

You will need: a bird table
variety of foods

Make or buy a bird table and set it up in a sheltered spot away from the danger of cats or vermin. Provide a variety of different foods, and always make sure there is water too. The children can be encouraged to observe and record the favourite foods of the different species of bird that visit the 'Bird Café', and also whether a greater variety of birds is attracted to the area as a result of setting it up. This activity will be particularly useful and rewarding during the winter months when many birds are desperate for food and water.

Birdtables should be cleared frequently, and occasionally scrubbed, to reduce the risk of salmonella poisoning which can be a threat to some species of birds.

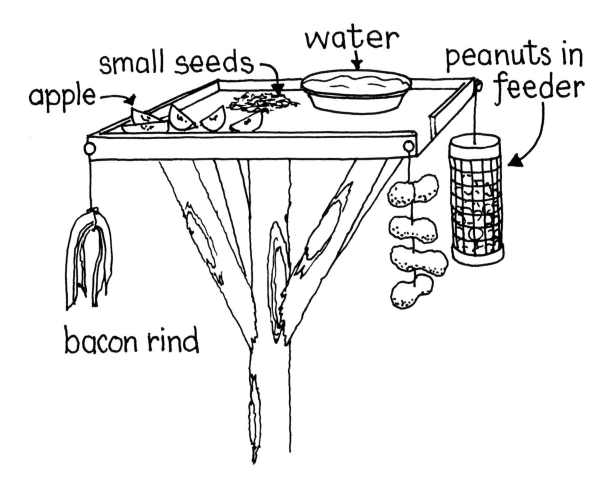

RECIPE FOR A BIRD CAKE
ADULT SUPERVISION ESSENTIAL!
Pour melted fat (suet or lard) onto a mixture of ingredients, such as wild bird seed, cake, nuts (finely chopped, unsalted), dried fruit, oatmeal and cheese. Use about one-third fat to two-thirds of the mixture.

Stir well in a bowl to bind the ingredients together, and when the mixture is solid, turn it out onto the birdtable.

ACTIVITIES

PLAIT MY HAIR

You will need: board, approx. 40cm x 50cm
cut-out, or hand-painted, faces

Decorate the board, as shown, with two faces and add collage materials as required. Glue lengths of the three colours of wool on to the board to cover the top and side of the heads.

At the nape of each neck, make a hole in the board and, using more lengths of the three colours of wool, push them through. Fasten to the back of the board with adhesive tape, leaving a good length hanging down the front.

The children can practise plaiting these strands of wool, and the three different colours of wool will help them to get used to the sequence of moves required in order to obtain a good plait.

reverse

knots of wool

ONE, TWO, FASTEN MY SHOE

Take a board of approx. 40cm square and paint it with a coat of emulsion paint. While this is drying, spray a pair of shoes or trainers in a well ventilated place, using gold or silver paint.

When these are dry, thread in some fluorescent laces. Decorate and label the board as shown, leaving space for the shoes. If you wish, cover the board with adhesive plastic film to protect it, and finally nail the shoes in place.

The children place the board on a table or on the floor so that they see the shoes in the same way as they would see their own feet when looking down at them. They can then practise tying their shoe laces.

SAILS IN THE WIND

Fill a water tray with water and let the children make a variety of model boats from margarine tubs or lids, or flat wooden shapes and blocks.

Use plastic straws for masts, held in place with adhesive putty, and cut different shaped paper sails to test.

Let the children experiment to see which shape of sail makes the boat move fastest, or in the straightest line, or go round in circles.

Which boat moves fastest?

CAR CITY

You will need: large cardboard boxes
radio-controlled or remote-controlled car
paint or paper

Use the large boxes to make houses and flats. First of all, paint the boxes or cover them with activity paper, and add details such as windows and doors. Add pitched roofs to the houses by folding rectangles of card and gluing these on to the boxes.

Roads chalked on playground

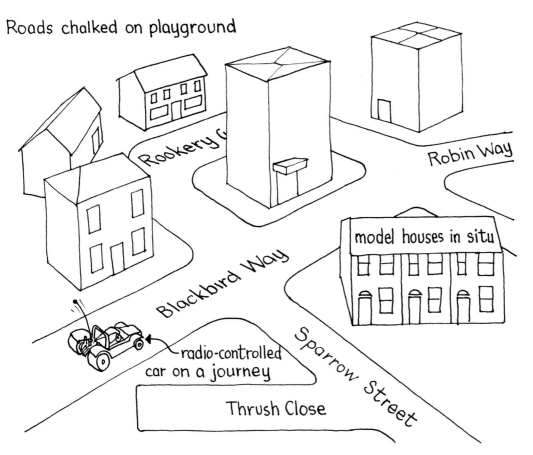

Use chalk to draw a street plan on the playground and put the buildings in place, as shown.

The children can take turns to negotiate a given route using the car.

For a more difficult task, let them try to work out a sequence of instructions for getting the car from one place to another.

51

PLANT GROWTH: LEAF BY LEAF

You will need: white card
felt-tip pens
bean seeds
cm ruler

On a large sheet of white card or stiff paper, mark the axes as shown, with the centimetres vertically on the left-hand side, and the plant pots as illustrated horizontally along the bottom.

The children observe the plant every day to see if there are any changes. These are recorded by drawing the plant on to the chart up to the correct height as shown by the centimetres on the vertical axis, while the day and date of the observation is recorded on the plant pot.

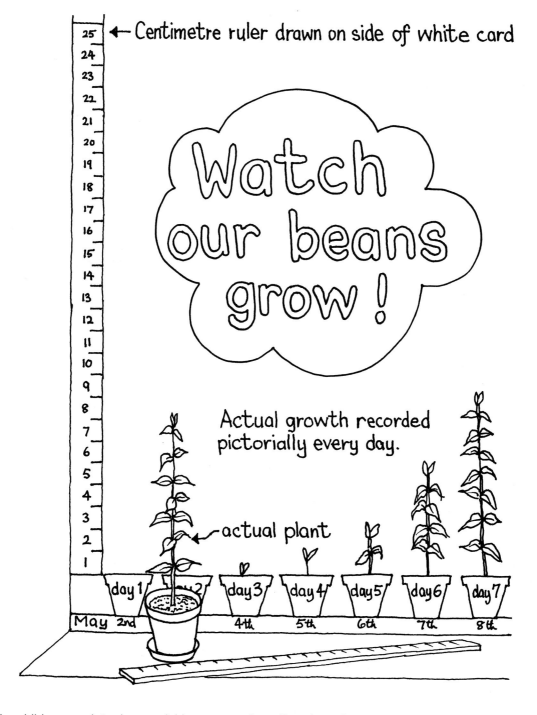

Older children can introduce variables to see what effect these have on growth, and an interesting comparison can be made between plants grown by various groups under different conditions in the classroom.

PLAYGROUND SUNDIAL

You will need:

    a vertical post in a baseboard
    (for example, a rounders post)
    chalk
    a sunny day

Go outside on a sunny day and place the post in a spot where no shadows are cast throughout the day. Draw a line around the base to fix the centre position.

On each hour, let the children go outside to mark with the chalk the place where the shadow is cast.

By the end of the day the sundial will be complete.

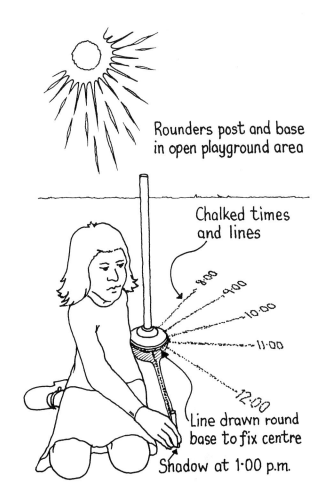

Rounders post and base in open playground area

Chalked times and lines

8·00
9·00
10·00
11·00
12·00

Line drawn round base to fix centre

Shadow at 1·00 p.m.

MOVABLE SUNDIAL

You will need:

    board cut to desired size
    glue gun
    compass
    dowel rod, approx 30cm
        long

Take the board, and shallow drill the centre to take the dowel rod. Fix this in place using the glue gun (remembering safety).

Alternatively, you can screw the rod in place with a screwdriver. Using a compass, plot the compass points and mark these in each corner as shown.

Using the same procedure as in the previous activity, mark off the hours on to the board with a felt-tip pen.

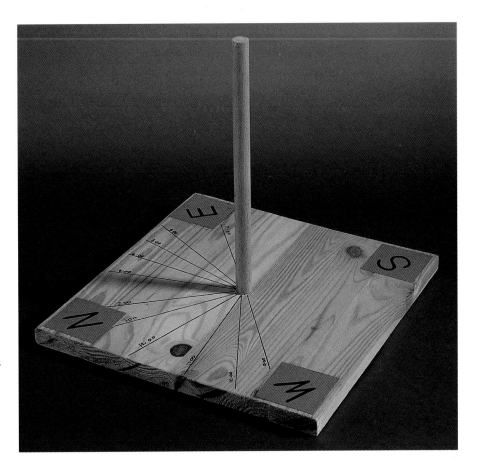

The words visible on the crafts:

Wood

hard
sharp bendy
non-bendy cold
shiny dull
hot warm
metallic

Metal

ha
rou
smelly
stron
spike
t

FEELY FACES TOTEM POLE
You will need:

> two very large cardboard
> boxes (for example,
> television or video)
> selection of different
> materials - plastic, wood,
> metal and fabric
> white paper
> coloured activity paper
> thick marker pen
> adhesive tape, glue

Paint or cover the boxes with coloured activity paper. Stack them vertically and glue them together (or use adhesive tape) to make the 'totem pole'. Put three or four house bricks inside the base box to stop it from falling over.

Make four faces using one of the different materials for each one: for example, one face made of metal scraps, another of plastic scraps, and so on.

Mount these on four sides of the boxes with accompanying text, as shown, to make a note of materials used, and relevant vocabulary.

Feely Faces - Plastic and Fabric - see facing page

MAGNET MODELLING
You will need:

> white card
> red and black paper
> coloured activity paper
> plastic cups
> Cellophane
> assorted metals and magnets
> large tray

Cover a wall or cupboard with activity paper. Cut out a large magnet shape from red paper and add two black ends as shown.

Take the white paper and cut out a force field shape larger than the magnet. Mount this on to backing card, then put the magnet shape in the middle of this. The space around the magnet shape can be used to write vocabulary.

Label as shown, and place the large tray in front of this and display the collection of different metals, magnets and materials.

The children can then build models which use the magnetic properties of the objects.

55

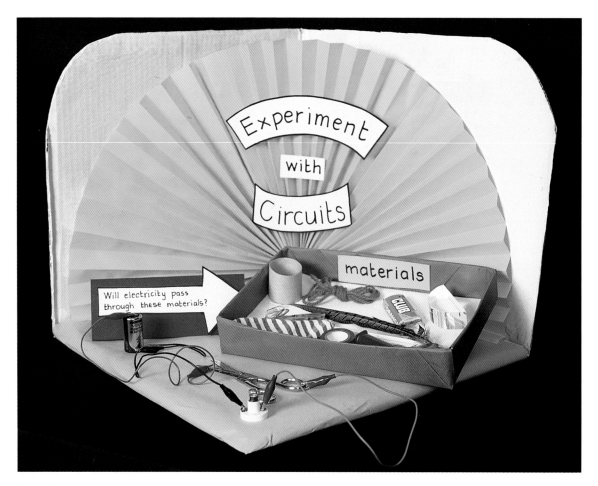

CIRCUITS

You will need:

yellow paper	adhesive putty
thick black felt-tip pen	fluorescent paper
batteries	wire
clips	tray or box lid
bulb and holder	variety of objects
white card	gold spray

Take a length of yellow paper and fold it like a concertina. Staple one end when folded, and open up like a fan. Fix this to the wall where you wish the display to be. Cut curved labels as shown and write in details with thick marker pen. Mount an arrow label on card folded into prism shape. Display a variety of objects to be tested inside the tray or box lid.

Finally, with the children, set up the circuit as shown and connect up the objects to the circuit with the clips. The children can test to see which objects conduct the current to enable the light to glow.

ELECTROMAGNETISM

You will need:

large flat box	white card
batteries	drawing pins, paper clips
small block of wood	metal bolt
copper wire	collection of different objects to be tested
piece of springy steel	

(See illustration on facing page)

Paint or cover the flat box with coloured activity paper and make a backdrop by cutting a sheet of the white card to fit across the back. Cut to shape and label as shown. Put the batteries, copper wire, bolt, wood and paper clips on the flat surface as illustrated and work with the children to set up the circuit and the switch. The children can then set up the experiment for themselves and test the collection of different objects to see which ones are attracted by the electromagnet.

(Setting up the experiment in this way means that all the components can be moved around very easily from group to group.)

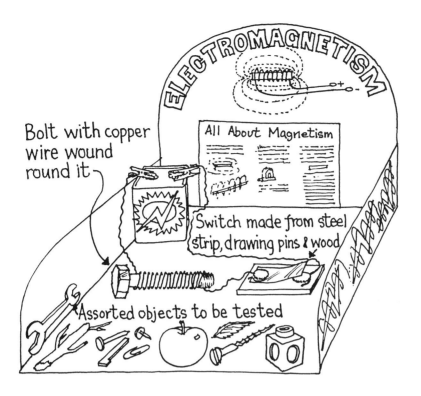

ELECTROMAGNETISM

Bolt with copper wire wound round it

All About Magnetism

Switch made from steel strip, drawing pins & wood

Assorted objects to be tested

Electromagnetism - see facing page

'FEED MY FACE'
You will need:

- medium size box
- wool
- paper
- plastic-covered wire
- spanner, or large nail or bolt
- piece of springy steel (to create the 'mouth')
- collection of different objects to be tested
- adhesive tape

Cover the box with activity paper (or paint it) and decorate it with cut-out eyes and nose. Glue on wool for hair to make it look like a head. Wrap the copper wire around the spanner and make two holes the width of this, just below the nose. Thread the ends of the copper wire through the holes to hold the spanner in place to create the mouth.

Set up the circuit in the space inside the box (see smaller photograph), and fix the 'head' to a baseboard or table-top with adhesive tape to stop it from falling over.

As before, the children can use the 'head' to test which things are attracted by the electromagnet by 'feeding' them to the bolt on the front of the head.

Feed me!

HANDS ON LIGHT

You will need:
- hologram card
- translucent tracing paper
- mirrors
- different coloured paper sheets
- blue or black paper
- torches
- transparent Cellophane
- binoculars

Cover the display area with the blue or black paper. Cut out large letters from the hologram card for the title. Cut circles of different colours from the coloured paper sheets, and decorate with frills made from the translucent tracing paper and the transparent Cellophane.

On one box, display torches and other objects, as shown. Above it mount shadow and silhouette drawings.

On the other box, place mirrors and silver foil. Display other objects, as shown, and encourage the children to make the kaleidoscope and periscope models to add to the display, and to try mirror writing and to complete symmetrical shapes.

A SIMPLE KALEIDOSCOPE

You will need:

3 lengths of mirror card, 20cm x 5cm
scraps of coloured paper and sequins

Attach the three strips of mirror card with adhesive tape as shown to make the kaleidoscope. Hold it over a pile of sequins and scraps of coloured paper, making sure that there is a light source to one side. (This could be light from a window or from a lamp.)

Turn the kaleidoscope to see the wonderful patterns created.

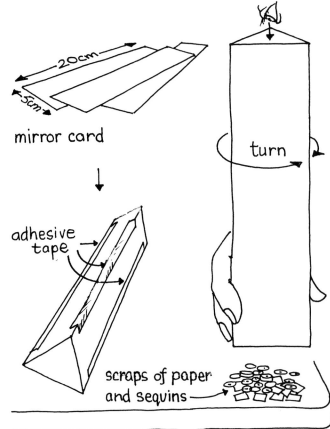

20cm

5cm

mirror card

adhesive tape

turn

scraps of paper and sequins

24cm

cut out square hole

50cm

① ② ③ ④

fold card and join to form cuboid

front of mirror

back of mirror

cut out square hole

score along bends

6cm

Light is reflected from one mirror to the other

A SIMPLE PERISCOPE

You will need:

thin black card 24cm x 50cm
two plastic mirrors
ruler, scissors

Divide the shortest side of the black card into four equal sections of 6cm. Score the lines and fold to make the cuboid. Cut a square hole in the top of the second section, and in the bottom of the fourth section, and cut two slits at an angle of 45 degrees in the first section and in the third section, making sure they are level (see illustration).

Fold the card, and strengthen the edges of the box with adhesive tape. Slide in the two mirrors as shown and secure with a little adhesive tape if necessary.

The periscope enables the children to see over the top of obstacles, provided they are not too high. After aiming the periscope, the children look into the bottom hole. The image from the other side of the obstacle is reflected from the top mirror to the bottom mirror where the children can see the reflection.

A BUS

The bus is best placed in a corner where the corrugated paper can be stapled to the walls. Use a cupboard or large box for the engine and place this in position as the front of the bus.

Make the body of the bus by running a length of corrugated card all around. Start by stapling to the back wall and extend the card along the side wall to the 'engine'.

Run the corrugated card across this, stapling as you go, then return to the back wall and staple in place as before.

Decorate the front box or cupboard to look like the engine. Make a foil-covered radiator, and paint on number plates. Paint two paper plates yellow for the headlights, and add two large circles of black card for the

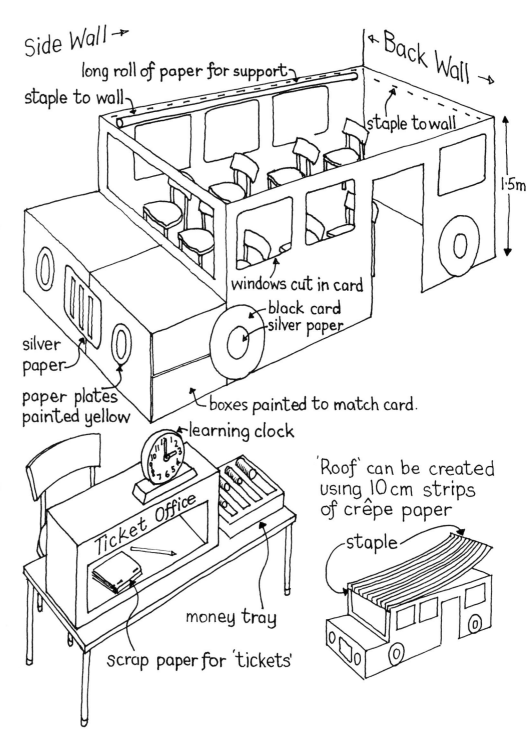

tyres, then add foil-covered paper plates for the hub caps. Cut windows in the sides as shown and put in classroom chairs for the seats.

You can make a roof for the bus in the same way as for the Flower Shop (see facing page), using strips of crêpe paper, first stapled to the wall then stapled to the top of the front of the bus (see illustration).

Add a simple ticket office by cutting a window in a shallow box and paint it and decorate with a sign. Attach this to a small table with adhesive putty or adhesive tape, and provide a chair.

Make timetables and price lists for destinations. Print tickets, provide a money tray and till, a large learning clock and note pad.

The children can pay for their tickets according to the price list. If you also include the number of minutes each journey takes, some children can perhaps work out times of arrival from a given departure time.

A FLOWER SHOP

If you have a three-sided playhouse, place it against a wall, as shown, with the open side out. Fix a length of dowelling or a long paper tube across the gap and cut strips of crêpe paper in colours of your choice.
Attach the strips of crêpe (using staples or adhesive tape) to the back wall, then create a sloping roof for the shop by fixing them to the cross piece as shown.

Use a large cardboard box or a small cupboard as the counter. Put on this a notepad and pencil, money tray and telephone, and a toy till.
Attach posters from florists' shops on the walls and cover old buckets and tins with coloured activity paper as flower holders.

Make wreaths and flowers as shown and place these all around to create a dazzling display of colour. Using price lists, the children will be able to make up bouquets and work out how much each costs. This will be determined by the price and number of the flowers contained in each one.

Containers cardboard carpet rolls painted

Shasta daisy white paper petals, stuck to base a yellow card centre on top.

Lilies a white paper cone, stapled to a green stem 40cm long

Stocks screwed-up balls of tissue paper stuck to a green stem 35cm long

Stems roll green paper from corner and secure with adhesive tape

Wreaths circles of pinched tissue, and green paper leaves on card ring

Palm Tree Foliage roll of green paper ← cut 12cm down roll, and pull up centre →

A SPACE CAPSULE

You will need:

table	corrugated card
large play tube	paper plates
wide roll of adhesive tape	silver foil
silver spray	shiny material for curtains
garden canes	

Cut a length of corrugated card long enough to fit around three sides of a table. Decorate the inside of the corrugated card with a control panel (as shown). The children can suggest the sorts of things to include. Use such things as plastic moulded wrapping material and chocolate box interiors with lots of shiny foil, and a variety of plastic bottle tops. Cut portholes in the other two sides.

Build 'Space Capsule' under a small low table, using cloth or corrugated card, taped round sides.

antenna →
rolled card 'arms'
shoe boxes
Tape tube to table legs
stiff card
paper plates
Play tube

Inside
Attach top to table, and bottom to floor

ZOOM SPACE roar orbit space planets
← window
computer + games

control panel details drawn or painted on large piece of card, or collage with plastic moulded wrapping or chocolate box interiors.

When completed, use adhesive tape to fix the corrugated sheet to the legs of the table and to the table-top. Cut two curtain lengths from the shiny material to fit over the open side of the table.

Also use adhesive tape to fix the large play tube to the side of one of the table legs and to the floor. Attach the other end of the tube to a nearby cupboard or table for good anchorage (see illustration).

The table-top can be decorated to look like a space capsule with antennae (garden canes sprayed silver), shoe boxes, and silver-sprayed paper plates as solar panels.

You could also put an old computer monitor inside, or site the actual class computer there, with a range of suitable games for the children to use once inside.

A VETERINARY SURGERY

Position a small desk near the front, as shown in the illustration, to act as the reception area, and place a till, money tray and perhaps an old computer keyboard on the top. Make a sign to show opening times and charges.

Arrange any other cupboards as desired to hold the dispensary or to accommodate other equipment such as washing-up bowl and towels, brushes and pan, or pet food.

Use a large cardboard box, painted or covered, as the operating table, and use smaller boxes or shelves as the animal hospital.

Place some of the animals on the shelves or stacked boxes as though they are waiting for, or recovering from, their treatment. As a finishing touch, place a sign over the top - and a selection of animal posters all around.

Alternatively, the children can design their own pet posters and advertisements for pet foods to decorate the surgery. Include a vocabulary list of things to look for at the 'Vet's'. This can be added to at any time and will help with any writing the children undertake.

NIGHT ADVENTURE

Place two tables together, as shown, and cut two lengths of corrugated card to fit the full length of the longer sides of the two tables. Attach these with wide adhesive tape to the inside of the tables. Decorate inside with children's paintings of night creatures.

Next, cut two lengths of material long enough to stretch the full length of the longest sides, and halfway across the two shortest sides. Fix to the table-top with a wide strip of tape. You will have a split in the material at each end of the tables to make an entrance and an exit.

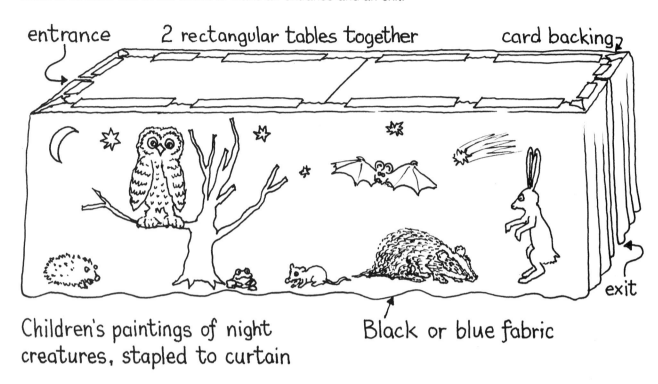

entrance   2 rectangular tables together   card backing

exit

Children's paintings of night creatures, stapled to curtain

Black or blue fabric

Decorate the outside with more children's paintings of night creatures stapled to the material.

Inside include two torches and a battery-operated tape recorder with story tapes so that the children have a place to read and listen to night-time stories. (This extra space created can also be used by a small group as stimulus for imaginative writing.)

A GHOST TRAIN

Measure a length of corrugated card to fit around three sides of a table. Cut out ghost shapes and skeleton shapes from white card, or paint directly on to the smooth side of the corrugated card.

Decorate both sides and fix strips of green plastic carrier bags. Cut hand shapes as shown - and attach to the inside surface of the corrugated card. Paint the title in bright fluorescent paints.

Wrap three sides of the table with the corrugated card, and attach this to the bottom of the table legs with adhesive tape.

Cut the black material to make two curtains on the open side. These can be fixed to the table-top with a wide strip of adhesive tape. You may decide to fix the other three sides to the table-top in the same way to prevent any light entering. Cover the joins with a strip of black paper glued to the top of the table.

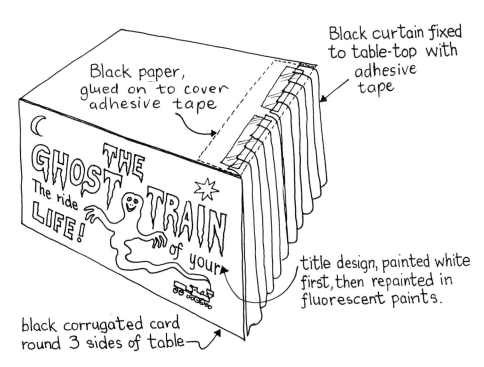

Black paper, glued on to cover adhesive tape

Black curtain fixed to table-top with adhesive tape

title design, painted white first, then repainted in fluorescent paints.

black corrugated card round 3 sides of table

Supply a battery-operated tape recorder and a couple of torches, together with story tapes, and the children will enjoy sitting in their spooky den to listen to, or read, the ghostly tales.

This theme may not be appropriate to use with the youngest children. It should, in any case, have a high level of supervision - and can be regarded as a very good opportunity for language development.

A WELCOME WAITING AREA

The entrance hall is a very important place in school, as it is very often the first thing that confronts visitors upon arrival. It is relatively easy to create an impression of warm welcome, with a minimum of expense.

You may be able to enlist the help of willing parents to help decorate the chosen spot, and although a matter of personal choice, the colours chosen will be very important.

Restful tones with a few splashes of bright colour may be more welcoming perhaps than an over-emphasis on primary colours.

The provision of comfortable seating with a small table will be well worthwhile, as it will provide visitors with a place to relax while waiting.

Fresh or dried flowers and healthy plants help to give a cared-for look, as does the provision of magazines or interesting books. For those occasions when parents with young children visit, a small chest of toys will help to occupy the children and pass the time.

Display children's work from all age groups on the walls and, if natural light is limited, highlight dark corners with subdued lighting from carefully positioned lamps. You could hang one special piece of children's work in a picture frame, changing it each month to give many children opportunity to 'star' in a public place.

If space allows, set aside an area where parents can park prams. Finally, add a simple sign saying 'Welcome to School'.

READING CORNER

The reading corner can be any size you wish, depending upon the amount of space in your classroom.

Rearrange the furniture to make an enclosed space, making sure that you can see into the area easily.

If you do not already have spare bookshelves for the reading corner, a simple low shelf can be created by placing a smooth plank of wood cut to size on top of clean house bricks, two at each end. This will be quite safe and stable if placed against a wall. Use two large coffee tins, filled with sand and decorated, as bookends.

The corner will be much more welcoming with the addition of a piece of carpet, plants, and some large scatter cushions - which can often be bought quite cheaply from local markets.

When choosing the position of the reading corner, try to choose a place with plenty of light. This could be near a window - but remember that even a short time sitting in the hot afternoon sunshine can be quite uncomfortable, so choose carefully.

Have a 'Book of the Week' spot to highlight particular stories or books related to a class topic, or any new books that become available. You can also display posters which some publishers will be delighted to let you have in return for a large stamped addressed envelope. Remember to change the books regularly, and encourage the children to bring in their favourite books from home to talk about and, perhaps, to swap with others.

Put in a tape recorder with headphones so that the children can listen and read, and encourage the children to make their own books for inclusion in the class library.

GARDEN AREA

A garden area can be created very inexpensively. Choose a suitable spot in the school grounds, relatively quiet with not too much through traffic, and decide on the sort of seating you want. A simple self-assembly bench available from DIY stores and supermarkets is not too expensive and can provide a focal point for a garden corner. Alternatively, you could use a set of children's patio chairs, or two or three redundant classroom chairs.

Placing a few tubs or pots of small shrubs and flowering plants around the seating will transform the area instantly. Choose the best pots you can afford to make the area as attractive as possible, but it is worth remembering that with the right planting even the cheapest pots can look good.

If you also provide a table, groups of children can be encouraged to work, read or play as an alternative to the sometimes rougher play of the school playground.

Encourage the children to bring in garden plants from home, if possible, and also encourage the children to look after, and take responsibility for, their garden - to keep it well watered and weeded.

Different classes could set up their own garden corners around the school grounds and this will result in an immediate improvement of the school environment.

If you wish to transform the school grounds as a whole, there are lots of organisations which will help you do this in terms of advice and planning, and many local authorities are keen to promote the idea of a 'green' school. Check what is available in your area.

HALL DISPLAY

This display brings together many of the elements found throughout this book: the niches, the rustic shelf, and the island of boxes - grouped together to make a display that the children have to look into and around to see the information presented.

The display was assembled to link with the creation of a school garden (see facing page), and the rustic arch was created using rolls of activity paper placed around the entrance to the school hall, so as the children pass through the arch each day they actually become a living part of the display.

NOTES

For details of further Belair publications,
please write to: Libby Masters,
BELAIR PUBLICATIONS LIMITED,
Albert House, Apex Business Centre,
Boscombe Road, Dunstable, LU5 4RL.

For sales and distribution (outside North America)
FOLENS PUBLISHERS
Albert House, Apex Business Centre,
Boscombe Road, Dunstable, LU5 4RL.
United Kingdom.

For sales and distribution in North America and South America,
INCENTIVE PUBLICATIONS,
3835 Cleghorn Avenue, Nashville, Tn 37215.
USA.

For sales and distribution in Australia
EDUCATIONAL SUPPLIES PTY LTD
8 Cross Street, Brookvale, NSW 2100.
Australia